Know About Drugs

Second Edition

Know About Drugs

Second Edition

by Margaret O. Hyde and Bruce G. Hyde

Illustrated by Bill Morrison

McGraw-Hill Book Company
New York • St. Louis • San Francisco • Auckland
Bogotá • Düsseldorf • Johannesburg • London • Madrid
Mexico • Montreal • New Delhi • Panama • Paris •
São Paulo • Singapore • Sydney • Tokyo • Toronto

Library of Congress Cataloging in Publication Data

Hyde, Margaret Oldroyd, date
   Know about drugs.

   SUMMARY: Describes various stimulants, hallucinogens, and barbiturates
and their effects on the body.
   1. Drugs—Juvenile literature. 2. Drug abuse—Juvenile literature.
[1. Drugs. 2. Drug abuse] I. Hyde, Bruce G., joint author. II. Morrison,
Bill. III. Title.
HV5801.H93   1979   613.8   79-13288
ISBN 0-07-031643-0

For Kirsten Ann Crowley

Contents

1.

New Ideas About Drugs

Information about drugs has been spreading from person to person for thousands of years. All around you there is news about drugs from those who have used them, from medical scientists, and from young people and old. You can get information from a television announcer, from a magazine, from a friend who has tried a drug, from a dealer who peddles heroin. You must decide who is the expert, who really knows about drugs.

Most of today's young people are smarter than any who have gone before them. They think for themselves. They search for the real facts. Their senses are tuned to what is happening, and many of them can sort the real happenings from the fakes.

The truth about drugs is hard to find. Do you believe friends who have tried drugs? Do you believe what you read? Do you believe what teachers say? Do you believe what your parents say? In all of these cases, the truth may not be what each of these people thinks. What they believe to be fact may be based on myth. Even the people who spend their lives studying drugs do not know the whole truth.

Certainly, finding out the truth about drugs is hard to do. Many young people of today feel that it is worth the trouble. This is especially true of those who are aware of yesterday's drug scene and know that today there are new ideas about many kinds of drugs.

Suppose someone offers you one of his favorite mind-expanding drugs. He claims it can do wonders. He wants you to share the great experience.

Perhaps you would take a long hard look at the situation. Should you take a drug just because he does? What will it do for you? What will it do to you? Do you need drugs to turn you on to life? Can you form your own opinion instead of borrowing one from a friend? This book will give you some information that can help you to know about drugs before you decide whether or not the drug offered is a drug you can safely take.

2.

What Is a Drug?

A drug is a chemical compound that is taken into the body. It may be used to prevent illness, to cure illness, to change feelings that are unpleasant, or to change feelings "just for fun." A drug may be helpful; a drug may be harmful.

Almost everyone is a drug-taker of sorts. Perhaps you never thought of tea, cocoa, and cola drinks as containing drugs that mildly affect the mind. One such drug is caffeine, and the drugs that people crave range from this one to heroin.

You have probably taken drugs that heal, or medicines such as aspirin, cough syrup, and penicillin at many times in your life. When you were a baby, your parents took you to the doctor for drugs to keep you well.

Suppose your dog has worms. They make him sick, and the dog's doctor wants to get rid of them. Suppose the doctor fed the dog a poison that would kill the worms. If the doctor did not use a special kind

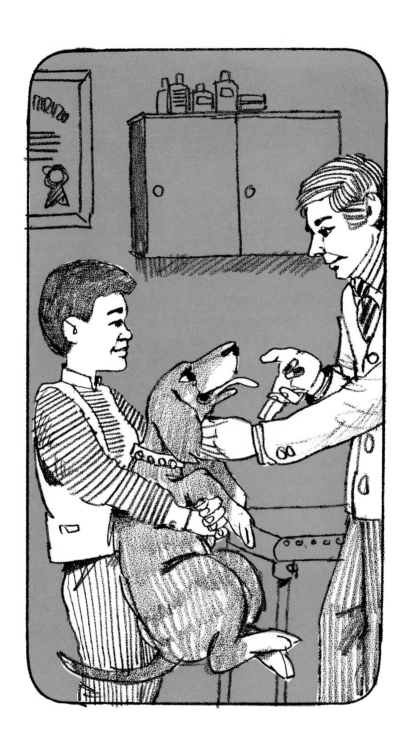

that poisoned worms and not the dog, your pet might die.

Drugs that are used as medicine are carefully tested in the laboratory before they are tried on people. Once a drug has been discovered, it must pass a great many tests. Even after years of testing, every drug carries some risk.

Since no *man-made* piece of machinery is as complicated as a living person, it is not surprising to find that there is much disagreement about the effects of drugs on the human body. This is especially true of drugs that affect the brain, for the human brain is the most complicated part of the living body.

3.

The World of Drugs

For people from seven to seventy, the world of drugs has many meanings. What happens to you when you take a drug? The answer to this question depends on many things, such as the amount of the drug, what kind of person you are, the kind of drug, and when and why the drug is taken.

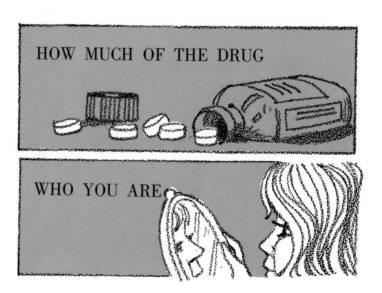

HOW MUCH OF THE DRUG

WHO YOU ARE

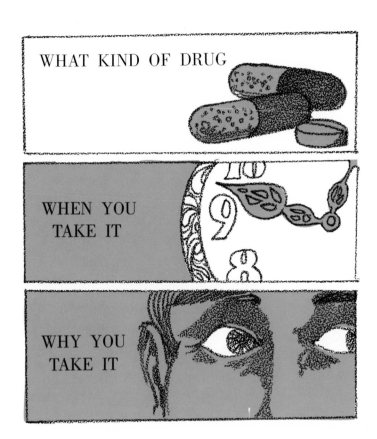

WHAT KIND OF DRUG

WHEN YOU
TAKE IT

WHY YOU
TAKE IT

4.

How Much?

At least one kind of medicine is advertised for almost every kind of ache and pain. If you have a headache, toothache, or earache, you probably take aspirin. If you have a cut, you put medicine on it to stop the pain and infection. Such drugs, used only when really needed, are very helpful. But many drugs are taken more often than is necessary. Drugs that are used for medicine and drugs that are used "for fun" can cause problems if one takes too much.

You might find it interesting to count the number of ads that you see or hear over a period of one week that encourage people to take a drug for some reason or other. If you see an ad repeated, count it again. Ads often tend to make people use things they don't need. Ads about drugs probably tell people to use drugs when they don't really need them. The use of drugs by a person who does not need them is usually called *abuse*.

People abuse drugs in a number of ways. They do

so when they use so much of a medical drug that it creates a problem for them. They do so when they use mood-changing drugs that may harm their bodies. They do so when they use any drug, legal or illegal, in such a way that it does not help them.

Drinking water is good for the human body, but too much water can kill a baby. The effect of tea on your mood, mind, and body chemistry depends on how strong the tea is. So it is with various substances that go into your body.

The effects marijuana has on a person seem to depend on how much is smoked or eaten, or how strong it is.

Drugs sold unlawfully are not always of the same strength. Many of the people who have taken overdoses of heroin thought they were using white powder that contained less of the pure heroin than it actually did. Sometimes, what is sold as a certain kind of drug has very little of that drug in it. In the case of illegal drugs, one never knows "how much."

5.

Who You Are

One of the most amazing things about your body is that it is different from any other human body in the world. This is one of the wonders of life. No one else is the same. You are one of a kind.

Have you ever stopped to think how exciting it is to be an individual? Through all the years that people have been living on this earth, no one has ever been quite like you. Around the world, there are four billion people living at this very moment. Not a single one of them is just like you.

Even if you have a twin brother or sister, he or she is different. You are alone in all the earth, in all the solar system, in all the universe. There is no one just like you on any other planet in the sky.

Each person has a different chemical makeup from anyone else, and this plays a part in how a drug will affect a person. When you take any medicine, the changes that take place in your body are not exactly like those that take place in another person's body when he or she takes the same medicine.

Take the case of Tony and Frank, who are twins. They look alike, weigh the same. Both have pneumonia. Tony is getting better quite fast with the help of the drug, penicillin. Frank cannot take this drug. Something in the chemistry of his body is different from that of Tony. Earlier tests showed that penicillin would make Frank very sick. Here a drug meant to cure would make him sicker than the disease it was meant to fight.

Even drugs as common as aspirin affect people differently. This is true because each person inherits a different body chemistry. Although millions of people take aspirin without bad effects, it does not agree with some people.

In one careful study, an exact amount of the drug, morphine, was given to twenty-nine healthy students. Eighteen had upset stomachs, sixteen went to sleep, nine felt drunk, thirteen felt giddy, nine complained of itching, and seven could not speak properly. Though there were only twenty-nine students, their various combined symptoms reached a total of seventy-two! You can see that each one was affected differently by the drug.

Who you are has much to do with what will happen if you take a drug. Since you are different from everyone else, taking a drug that is a help to someone else may be a risk for you.

6.

Which Drug?

Are there people with certain kinds of personalities who are attracted to special kinds of drugs? Some may crave excitement, some may want to escape from problems, and some may be searching for a religious experience, and so on. No one knows the whole story of why a person chooses to abuse one drug rather than another, or even to abuse any drug. Perhaps it has much to do with the friends one makes.

Certainly there are many kinds of drugs that are used and abused. Let's discuss some of them.

1. MARIJUANA

Although marijuana has been a common drug in many countries for thousands of years, the reports about what it does in the human body still do not agree. In the United States, millions of dollars have been spent and years of time have been used in a search that has not provided all the answers.

21

Marijuana comes from a weed called hemp, known since ancient times. Scientifically, it is called *Cannabis sativa*. It will grow in almost any climate with little or no care. The strength of the marijuana that is smoked is not always the same. Combinations of chopped marijuana leaves, flowers, and stems are common.

The active part of the plant, which changes a person's mood, or produces the "high" feeling, is a compound that scientists call tetrahydrocannabinol, or THC. The marijuana that is smoked in the United States contains various amounts of this substance. The female plant secretes a substance, something like varnish, that contains more THC than the usual marijuana that is smoked. In India, this strong preparation is known as charas, and in the Arab world, it is known as hashish.

In order to learn more about how marijuana affects the body, many scientists have experimented with known strengths of marijuana grown on farms that are controlled by the government. They agree on some of the actions of the active drug, THC, in the body. They know that it passes from the lungs directly into the blood. The heart beats faster and the eyes may redden. In addition to these physical changes, most users experience pleasant feelings. Some giggle, feel happy, and talk more than usual.

Authorities know that higher doses may cause confusion and drowsiness. Individuals cannot remember things as well while they are feeling very high, but old memories still remain intact when the effects wear off. A half hour may seem like an hour, but this effect is temporary, too.

Authorities disagree about long-term effects. It is difficult to measure whether or not heavy use of marijuana causes the user to lose interest and ambition. Some medical scientists claim that heavy use may cause damage to the liver and brain and reduce the body's ability to fight off disease. Others disagree. Many researchers believe that the smoke may be harmful to lungs. Until a drug is used on a large scale for a great number of years, one cannot be certain about long-term effects.

One thing is certain. Studies show that people who drive while high are more likely to be involved in accidents than when they are not intoxicated. Many marijuana users still do not know that they cannot drive a car well after smoking.

In many countries of the world, marijuana is an illegal drug. Laws that caused marijuana users to be jailed have been changed in some parts of the United States. There is still much indecision about how to discourage the use of the drug without tagging the offender with the stigma of a criminal record. In some states, a person who owns a small amount of marijuana is punished only by a fine, but this is not true everywhere.

As laws become less strict, some authorities are

concerned about the use of stronger marijuana in the United States. Now more of this drug comes from Colombia, South America. Colombian marijuana may contain three to ten times as much THC as that grown in Mexico, a source of most marijuana in the past. When scientists conduct new tests with the marijuana of increased strength, new results may add to the confusion about the effects of marijuana on the human body.

2. ALCOHOL

One of the most popular drugs in the world is alcohol, although many people do not think of it as a drug. Alcohol is probably the oldest mood changer, dating back to the early Stone Age. At some times in history, people used it to put themselves to sleep for medical reasons as well as for the pleasant feelings it can produce.

What happens when a person drinks an alcoholic beverage? The answer to this question depends on many things, especially the amount of alcohol in the drink. One bottle of beer, one glass of wine, and one drink containing one ounce of gin, vodka, or other liquor contain about the same amount of alcohol. Many people think they cannot get drunk on a few bottles of beer, but this is not true. "It's only a beer" is a misleading statement.

When alcohol reaches the walls of the stomach and the small intestines, it goes directly into the bloodstream. The blood carries it to the brain in a short period of time.

While low doses of alcohol stimulate, high doses slow down the area of the brain that governs judgment and thought. Alcohol gives some people feelings of power and great mental ability. At high doses it interferes with coordination (body movements) and thinking.

Relaxed feelings occur with small amounts but with large amounts there may be a drunken feeling, and if drinking continues, a person may "pass out." In some cases, the drinker becomes violent or depressed.

At some time in your life, you will probably have to decide whether or not you want to try alcoholic beverages. About one third of the people in the United States choose not to drink. Some do so for religious reasons. Many prefer to relax without the use of drugs for different reasons.

Many young people begin to drink because their friends pressure them to join the group. Those who decide to drink may find it helpful to learn as much as they can about this drug before they experiment with it.

While the use of the drug, alcohol, may be a pleasant social experience for most adults, about one person out of ten suffers from a drinking problem that

causes tremendous upsets in his or her way of life and
that of their families. Heavy drinking can damage the
heart, the stomach, the liver, and the brain.

The decision you make about drinking alcohol—
whether to, when, how much—may have an important influence on the course of your life.

3. COCA AND COCAINE

Cocaine comes from coca leaves that are part of a plant that is grown commonly in the high mountains of Bolivia and Peru. Coca is different from cocoa, a substance found in chocolate. Generations of South American Indians have chewed coca leaves to help them endure difficult working conditions at high altitudes. In addition to supplying small amounts of the drug, coca, the leaves provide them with some vitamins and minerals.

Eduardo is a boy of your age who works long hours in the fields. He and more than a million other Indians chew coca leaves for religious, medicinal, and work-related reasons. You probably would not enjoy chewing coca leaves since it takes a great deal of chewing to feel any effect.

Some of the richer people in South America and in other countries use cocaine, a white powder that is made from the coca leaves. In its pure form, cocaine has a variety of effects on the human body. Some users report a sense of physical and mental well-being and reduced fatigue. A common reaction is feeling like a very powerful person who can solve any problem. This is followed by a time of feeling sad and depressed. After using large quantities, some users tell of shaking all over, and fearing people and things that do not exist. Brain damage is being found among Bolivians who smoke cocaine paste or inhale a nearly pure form of the drug.

In the United States, cocaine is both illegal and so expensive that much of it is mixed with impurities to stretch it. One of the dangers of cocaine sniffing is not knowing what these impurities are. They may be far more harmful than the drug itself.

Not many sniffers can afford enough cocaine to cause holes in the partitions of their noses, but there have been enough cases of this nose damage to concern doctors about possible ways of repairing it. Still, people disagree about how many users suffer damage to the wall between the nostrils.

Why do people continue to use cocaine in spite of the threat of severe legal penalties? Heavy users experience an intense craving for the drug and the feelings it brings. The craving for cocaine may be great but it is the powerful stimulating effect of cocaine and the impurities mixed with it that makes many doctors consider cocaine a very dangerous drug.

4. CIGARETTES

Karen is a pollution fighter in the Green Mountains of Vermont. Each spring, when the snow begins to melt from the slopes, she and other Vermonters clean away the trash that the skiers have tossed between the layers of snow. All year long, Karen fights another kind of pollution. She fights the drug, nicotine, and the tars and carbon monoxide that pollute lungs and whole bodies.

Karen's father grew up when it was considered smart to smoke cigarettes. He forgets the real smell of freshly mowed lawns and of spring flowers. He does not even notice the smell of stale cigarettes in his clothing and in the rooms where he has been smoking. These odors bother Karen, but cigarettes have dulled her father's sense of smell.

After Karen's father began to smoke, he used more spices on his food. He likes tacos with extra hot sauce. He keeps hoping something will wake up his sense of taste. All that he needs to do is stop smoking. Then his senses of taste and smell will return to normal.

Stopping the cigarette habit is not easy for most people. Karen's father does not think of himself as a drug addict, but he has tried to stop smoking a number of times. Each time, he suffers chills and dizziness. His hands have the habit of reaching for a cigarette. His body is used to nicotine.

Karen has given her father a list of suggestions that may help him stop smoking. They include: planning two weeks ahead to stop on a certain day; making a record of all the cigarettes smoked in one day and trying to smoke half that many on each day that follows; making a pact with another smoker to stop all at once; going to a clinic that has a program for people who want to break the smoking habit.

The message about the dangers of nicotine is being spread in many ways. Young people such as Karen

are playing an important part in helping others to know the truth about this drug. They are more aware of possible dangers to their lungs and hearts than the young people of previous generations. They even consider the opinion of some scientists who believe that smoking can reduce the desire for healthful activity. They take pride in being in control of their own health.

5. PCP (ANGEL DUST)

One of the most popular drugs for changing feelings is called by many names. PCP, angel dust, crystal, elephant tranquilizer, goon, busy bee, and hog are some of them. Its scientific name is phencyclidine. Many doctors who have helped users who have had bad experiences call it a terror drug. The effects are so uncertain, that PCP has also been called heaven and hell.

PCP is an inexpensive drug that was found unsafe for use as an anesthetic and limited to use by veterinarians. It is often used as a filler with more expensive illegal drugs. Sometimes it is sold as THC, the active ingredient in marijuana, and as "super grass" when it is mixed with marijuana in cigarettes. Its identity is hidden in many other ways, too.

Whether PCP is snorted, swallowed, injected or smoked, it can produce strange effects. After taking a

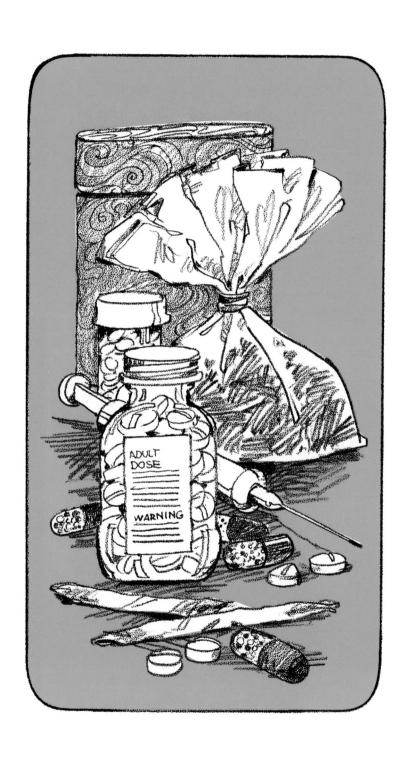

small amount, the user feels changes in body awareness. The mind might feel separate from the physical body. With increased doses, mental confusion usually occurs. Illusions (sensing the world in a distorted way) and hallucinations (hearing and/or seeing things that are not there) are common. PCP is classed as a hallucinogen.

Not all people feel the same way after taking PCP even when the amounts are similar. Some enjoy pleasant feelings. Others become very violent, even killing other people or themselves. Still others act in many different ways. The same person may have very different experiences after each use.

In one case, a 13-year-old boy and a 14-year-old boy sucked and chewed a lump of white "crystal" during a basketball game, and both went into comas. One boy awoke after four hours, but he continued to have hallucinations for several days. The other boy did not awaken for four days. He suffered severe convulsions and his hallucinations lasted for six days after he woke up. Doctors believe that the effects of this drug last so long because the PCP is recycled in the body.

No one knows what will happen when PCP is taken. It is known that about one third of the people reporting to drug treatment centers have tried PCP and one fifth are regular users.

6. SNIFFING

Someone finds a chemical that makes him feel lightheaded when he sniffs it. He sends along the information to a friend. Paint, aerosol products, glue, gasoline, and petroleum products are some of the things that people, ranging in age from six to sixty, try in their efforts to use "fumes for fun."

Now and then someone sniffs too much or too often. Now and then someone has the kind of body chemistry that reacts violently to a certain sniffing drug. Serious illness, or even death, may result from some chemicals.

Fred inhales "poppers" (butyl nitrate) ten to twenty times during an evening of disco dancing. He admits that sometimes he feels as if his brains are going to fall out. Sometimes he cannot stand up. Those are the nights when he uses his inhaler too often. Fred says he has thought about the bad effects of the butyl nitrate he uses, but he gets good feelings from it and he does not stop.

Doris has stopped sniffing. One night she had to be taken to the emergency room of the hospital. In addition to the scare she had, Doris was tired of the headaches that came after sniffing.

Long-term effects from sniffing include tiredness, loss of appetite, shaking, bad breath, and forgetfulness. Some chemicals produce serious changes that may not be noticed immediately, such as changes in

bone marrow, blood cells, kidneys, liver, and brain. Now and then, effects are dramatic. One cooking spray for pans can literally glue the lungs shut to incoming air. Several deaths have been reported from this. Records show more than one hundred deaths in one year from sniffing.

The list of possible dangers from sniffing is long, even though many have been highly exaggerated. In some cases, the smell of the chemical is the worst punishment. Some former sniffers have found that they can enjoy the scent of flowers more than the chemicals they used to try.

7. HEROIN

Heroin is a drug that is produced from morphine, a pain-killing medicine that is made from the juice of the unripe opium poppy. Heroin was developed by a drug company as a pain killer and cough medicine, and it was used as a cure for morphine dependence until it was discovered that heroin, too, is addictive.

Heroin, morphine, and opium are all known as opiates. They have similar effects on the body, such as depressing the central nervous system, making a person feel at peace with the world, decreasing pain, producing constipation, and all change body chemistry and are addictive. All are considered heavy, or dangerous, drugs.

Several hundred thousand people in the United

States who heard the message that heroin is a dangerous drug used it anyway. The story of George is a typ-
ical case.

At the insistence of a friend, George tried sniffing
heroin. He enjoyed the tingling sensation in his nostrils and the way it made his troubles disappear. He
forgot the argument he had with his mother that
morning. The money he owed his sister was also for-
gotten. He stopped worrying about school for a while.
After chatting with the friend who had introduced
him to the drug, he had a nice nap.

The next day George was somewhat annoyed with
himself for having tried a drug that he knew could
become a dangerous habit, but he decided he would
not try it more than a few times, and that would be
safe enough. The few times went by, and then George
tried it for a few more. Each time he meant it to be
the last time. He was sure he could stop before things
went too far, before he needed the drug the way some
of his friends did, in order to live comfortably.

One morning George awoke feeling awful. He
sniffed a bit of the white powder and felt better again.
This happened many times before George admitted to
himself that he needed the heroin. Soon this drug became the most important thing in his life. He wanted
help, but his friends could not give it to him. George
had increased the doses. He used larger amounts by
"mainlining" (injecting the drug into a blood vessel).
The scars showed on his arm.

40

George had stolen money from his family to supply
the ever-increasing amount of heroin he needed to
keep him feeling well. He had done many things of
which he was ashamed. But he did not, and could not,
stop. When he was deprived of his drug, the with-
drawal pains made life very unpleasant. He could not
cope with the problem.

George enjoyed the immediate pleasure that he received from the heroin. He preferred it to working
slowly, day after day, with little or no satisfaction in
what he was doing. The drug helped him to face life
today, even though it meant larger problems to-

morrow. Before long, it seemed to become life itself.

Do you think George was stupid? He was not so different from many people who believe "getting hooked" cannot happen to them. Almost everyone feels this way about certain things. Many people who smoke believe that cigarettes are related to lung cancer, but they feel, "It won't happen to me."

George wanted to be one of the group. Unfortunately, he picked the wrong group, and became a victim of heroin.

Today, George is one of the fortunate heroin addicts. He has been taken into a program in which another drug, methadone, is used to block his craving for heroin. This drug is addictive too, but he does not need increasingly greater amounts in order to prevent discomfort. Methadone has been compared to the drug insulin, which a diabetic must use because his own pancreas does not secrete a sufficient supply of insulin. Of course, methadone is not necessary for life the way insulin is. Some doctors believe that it can be used to help an addict until he learns a new way of life and then it can be safely stopped. Others disagree.

In the case of heroin, a person's body chemistry can become so changed that he cannot be comfortable unless its use is continued, or a substitute drug is used to replace it. "Hot lines," telephone centers where volunteers wait for calls from troubled drug users twenty-four hours a day, are the beginning of long-range help for many who want to free themselves of the heroin habit. In some cases, long-term therapy seems to be making it possible for addicts to make deeper friendships and find a better life. Ex-addicts often play a part in helping heroin users to rebuild their personalities so that they can cope with their problems in a world free of all drugs, from nicotine to scag (heroin).

The best way to be sure that you do not become an addict who is dependent upon such a drug is never to try it. Fortunately, most of today's young people know this. And they understand that such addiction is an illness, rather than a crime. Today's young people play an important part in spreading the message that "scag alley" is usually a dead end.

8. OTHER DOWNERS

Downers are chemical ways of getting low. Heroin and alcohol are examples. Other drugs that slow down body processes and dull the senses include barbiturates, methaqualone, and a wide variety of tranquilizers. Many people who get downers from doctors have a habit of taking them. Some go from one doctor to another for their prescriptions. If they take enough downers for a long enough time, the habit can be both physical and emotional. When these people stop, their bodies must adjust to being without the chemicals. In the case of barbiturates, the body may go into convulsions when the regular drug supply is stopped.

Most people who take drugs prescribed by doctors do not form serious habits. This may be true of people who buy their drugs illegally, too. But illegal supplies can vary a great deal in strength as well as in the impurities they include.

Barbiturates in the drug underground are known as goof balls, yellow jackets, red devils, red birds, blue heavens, pink ladies, and by many other names. Either alone, or in combination with other drugs, barbiturates account for a high percentage of drug-related problems.

Methaqualone is prescribed under the names of

Quaaludes, Soper, Optimil, Parest, and Somnifac but common names are more plentiful. Quads, quas, soper, super soper, soaps, ludes, and so on are variations of the names of the medicines. Methaqualone was once considered safe and non-habit forming, but

45

it was learned that this is not the case. When abusers resist the urge to sleep, the relaxation of their bodies makes walking and talking difficult. (The term "wall-banger" applies to abusers bumping into walls.)

Tranquilizers include a wide variety of drugs that depress the central nervous system. Doctors write millions of prescriptions for these drugs each year. They are especially dangerous when combined with alcohol. All combinations of downers can be dangerous.

Picture a rock singer relaxing after a concert. He has an alcoholic drink, then pops a few barbiturates into his mouth. This does not relax him enough, so he takes a few more. Now his mind is so confused that he cannot remember how many pills he has taken. It is easy to take a few more. The barbiturates produce vomiting, which might make him choke to death.

9. UP, DOWN, AND AWAY

"Ups" and "downs" and other combinations of drugs are tried by many users who are playing games with their feelings. Take the case of Mary. She is a gentle girl who was introduced to many kinds of drugs through friends. She became restless and ran away from home. Now she is a "speed freak," the slang for someone who injects large doses of drugs, called amphetamines, directly into the bloodstream. Immediately Mary feels a "rush." She is cheery, more alive, and there is blood pounding through her body, especially in her head. In a few minutes this feeling changes to a "high." Her body is flooded with physical and mental energy, and she talks and talks.

Mary has taken a drug which is called a stimulant, or an "up." After the "up," Mary will "crash," or come down. Sometimes Mary takes barbiturates to come down from her "high," so she will not feel quite so awful. Soon, though, she is sad and tired. So she will again lift herself by another injection of speed. Then she is on a cycle of speed and barbiturates, of "ups" and "downs."

Mary's future is not very bright. The chemicals she puts in her body may damage her brain. These drugs may cause her to live in a world that seems continually unreal. She may go without food for several days. She may have feelings that make her believe that people are spying on her. Mary may even die from a combination of lack of food for her body and exhaustion.

Mary's future may depend on other young people who know the facts about drugs. The bright young people of today may help her to turn on in creative ways, and to replace her lonely feelings. They may teach her to get her "highs" in just being with friends, talking with them, feeling joy with them.

Amphetamines, a type of upper, are listed by some treatment programs as the drug posing the most serious single abuse problem. Doctors have been dis-

couraged from using them as diet pills, and in some states, it is against the law for them to do so. Although amphetamines lessen appetite for a short while, they soon lose this effect. Higher and higher doses are needed to accomplish the same purpose. Amphetamines cause the heart and other body systems to race at a high speed. The user may feel capable of superhuman feats, while the body uses its stored energy until it is so low that the user gets a headache and also feels tired, frightened, confused, and dizzy. Even when sleep comes, it is not normal and refreshing. Barbiturates do not really cancel out amphetamines.

The number of prescriptions for amphetamines has decreased with new controls, but many of these drugs are made illegally and sold under names such as bennies, black beauties, dexies, meth, pep pills, and speed. Many people have heard the slogan "Speed Kills."

10. OTHER HALLUCINOGENS

In addition to PCP, drugs such as psilocybin, LSD (lysergic acid diethylamide), and peyote are called hallucinogens. They make a person's brain report things that do not exist. The user sees, hears, feels, and tastes in a way that is not the usual way. Sometimes these senses seem mixed, so that a person seems to smell sounds or hear tastes. With hallucino-

gens, one experiences unreal feelings. Sometimes the "trip" is very wonderful; sometimes it is very terrible.

What will happen if you take a drug such as LSD? Here again, the *kind* of drug plays only a part—along with the who, how much, when, and why. Thousands of thrill-seekers have found the taking of drugs no more than an exciting way to pass the time. For many, though, it has meant horror; for some it has meant death.

Perhaps you have read stories of people who have taken LSD and believed that they could fly. They have walked out of high windows or stepped from cliffs. Other users have unexpected and unwanted "trips" from drugs taken as long as a year before, and they never know when they may have another one.

The list of drugs that affect the mind is growing faster than scientists are finding out exactly what drugs do to the human body. Certainly some can cause damage to the brain, liver, spinal cord, and other organs. Some, sold as hallucinogens, may be as harmless as banana peel, or "68," which turned out to be oil of peppermint.

Drugs that were once tagged as "mind expanders" are being studied today with greater caution and these days fewer people who know about drugs are willing to try hallucinogens.

7.

When?

What happens when your body takes in a certain amount of a drug may depend partly on when you take it. Some people talk about this as the "set," or setting. Actually, the place, the people around you, your mood at the time are all part of the "set."

On Wednesday, John drank the same amount of alcoholic beverage that he had drunk on Tuesday. On Tuesday, it had barely affected his mood, for he had eaten well, was rested, and had drunk slowly in the presence of friends. On Wednesday, John was depressed, he was tired, he had not eaten much, and he drank to escape from his troubles. His body reacted very differently from the way it had the day before.

"Set" has much to do with many drugs. In tests with marijuana, some people experienced the effects that they expected to have from the drug even though they were given none. They did not know that what they had smoked was not marijuana and they really felt "high." Some of the people in the experiment, who were frightened about smoking the drug, had an unpleasant time. This often happens when marijuana is smoked illegally, as well as in experiments.

The kind of "trip" one has with hallucinogens may depend on the conditions under which one takes the drug, but this does not always seem to be the case. Some doctors who once acted as guides in medical experiments with LSD are afraid to experiment with the drug because the when, why, how much, and what kind do not *always* determine what will happen. Even they do not know all the answers. They cannot always guess what it will do to any human brain.

8.

Why?

Why plays a part in how the human body handles some of the drugs people take. People who are given narcotics for medical reasons seem less apt to become addicted than those who use them for escape. However, many people become drug abusers after taking drugs prescribed by doctors. This is especially true of people who take more medicine than the doctor orders and of people who get medicine from several doctors. People who drink alcoholic beverages to celebrate happy times may be able to control the reaction better than those who feel tired, anxious, and depressed, and drink because they "need" a drink. But those who combine prescription drugs with alcohol are in special danger of bad reactions and of becoming addicted.

Marijuana smokers and some other drug users seem to fall into several groups. One includes those who try a drug once or twice as an adventure or because they are curious, but then find other ways of enjoying themselves. A second group uses drugs socially, either legally or illegally. They do not make them a central part of their lives.

The people who abuse drugs are those who depend on them heavily as a crutch to escape their problems. They form a third group. The drugs increase the problems rather than solve them. So it is that the professional people who are attempting to help drug abusers try to do more than just break their drug habits.

How much, who you are, what kind of drug, when and why you take a drug, all play a part in how good or bad a drug can be for your body. Whether they heal, provide pleasure or trouble—great or small—depends partly on your knowing the facts.

9.

You Can Make Your Own Decisions

More and more young people are helping their generation make an honest search for a better future and real values. More and more are trying to communicate with each other in better ways.

Anyone can join in the world of drug abuse. It has been called the "fraternity of the hopeless." The drug abusers have been called "the lonely empties," for they seem unable to make deep friendships. They use a chemical crutch that may bring instant ecstasy, but may bring permanent trouble.

The young adults of tomorrow know more than the adventurers, the lonely, the troubled, the curiosity seekers who today search for magic in a pill.

They know that there are lonely times in every person's life. There are times when each person wishes he or she could be closer to other people in his family. There are times when they wish they could be closer to their friends. They want to feel that they are

part of a larger group. Everyone feels this way at some time.

When one reaches the age of eleven or twelve, feelings of loneliness may become especially strong. Everyone wants to be like everyone else, to wear the same clothes, and to do the same things. Being alone and being different does not seem to be a good thing.

This is true for everyone, although some people feel more deeply about it than others.

Strangely enough, some of the people who most dislike being different and being alone are those who admire a man named Thoreau. He stood against the world for what he believed, even though he was different. One of his remarks has become much admired by many young people, as well as by people of many different ages:

"If a man does not keep pace with his companions, perhaps it is because he hears a different drummer. Let him step to the music which he hears, however measured or far away." (*Walden—The Pond in Winter*)

All people look for substances or methods of changing their state of awareness and increasing their pleasure. Some do it by meditation, massage, or by learning to relax so they are neither fully asleep or awake. Some find a variety of drugless ways. For those who choose drugs, knowing the toxic effects can be very important. Some drugs are far more toxic than others.

Some young people ask:

WILL IT TURN YOU ON. . . .
OR WILL IT TURN ON YOU?

Even in colleges, many students who have tried drugs are looking around for answers that drugs did not give them. Drugs did not make their problems go away. Some of them are saying that drugs are "anti-life," and they want to be involved in the real world.

Rather than turning on and turning *in,* the new "turn-on" is finding meaning in life by becoming involved. The new scene is a non-drug one, where sharing both the hopes and pains of others is more important than the ownership of things or the turning off of life by the use of chemicals.

Many of tomorrow's high-school students are learning the facts about drugs. They know the difference between use and abuse. They enjoy changes of mood, but they like always to be in control. It is no longer smart to try new kinds of drugs to see what happens. Those who KNOW ABOUT DRUGS know that it is no longer smart to play with one's own brain.

Index

About the Author

MARGARET O. HYDE is the author of an outstanding list of nonfiction books for young readers. Mrs. Hyde earned a master's degree at Columbia University and received an honorary doctor of letters degree from Beaver College, her alma mater. Her recent books include *My Friend Wants to Run Away; Everyone's Trash Problem: Nuclear Wastes; Know About Alcohol;* and *Addictions: Gambling, Smoking, Cocaine Use and Others.* Margaret Hyde and her husband live in Burlington, Vermont.